How to Conquer Your Goliaths

SHEPHERD'S
VOICE

How to Conquer Your Goliaths

7 Keys to Overcome Every Problem That Prevents You from Reaching Your Dreams

Bo Sanchez

#1 Bestselling Author of *How to Turn Thoughts Into Things*

Other Books by Bo Sanchez:

Inspirational
How to Live a Life of Miracles
40 Stories of Passion
Don't Worry, Be Happy
How to Turn Thoughts into Things
How to Conquer Your Goliaths
5 Things You Need to Do Before You Die
My Conspiracy Theory
How to Be a Blessings Magnet

Personal Finance Series
8 Secrets of the Truly Rich
8 *Sikreto Para Maging Tunay na Mayaman*
Simplify and Live the Good life
Simplify and Create Abundance
8 Habits of the Happy Millionaire
My Maid Invests in the Stock Market
The Turtle Always Wins

Kerygma Collection
How to Be Really, Really, Really Happy (1st Collection)
You Can Make Your Life Beautiful (2nd Collection)
You Have the Power to Create Love (3rd Collection)
Fill Your Life with Miracles (4th Collection)

Inner Healing Series
Your Past Does Not Define Your Future
Stop Hidden Addictions
Awaken the Healer in You

Singles & Relationships
How to Find Your One True Love
How to Find Your One True Love, Book 2
40 Stories of Finding Your One True Love
How to Build a Happy Family

Children's Book
Eagles Don't Fly, They Soar!

Bo's Websites:
Read Bo's Blogs at **www.BoSanchez.ph**
Watch Bo's Videos at **www.PreacherInBlueJeans.com**
Get Daily Spiritual Food at **www.KerygmaFamily.com**
Gain Financial Abundance at **www.TrulyRichClub.com**
Receive Daily Messages at **www.GodWhispersClub.com**

Dedication

My secret to conquering Goliaths is my dream team.
And through the years, God has added new champions
into my life.
I dedicate this book to the newer builders of my spiritual family,
Light of Jesus (in alphabetical order):
Alvin Barcelona, Randy Borromeo, Obet Cabrillas,
Jorge Diomampo, Jon Escoto, Vic Español, George Gabriel,
Arun Gogna, Rudy Mallari, Adrian Panganiban, Eng Si
and Marvin Tan.
Thank you for being my dearest brothers
and faithful companions.
I'm a champion because of you.

How to Conquer Your Goliaths

7 Keys to Overcome Every Problem That Prevents You from Reaching Your Dreams

ISBN- 978-971-007-009-1
BO SANCHEZ

Philippine Copyright © 2009 by Eugenio R. Sanchez, Jr.
3rd Reprinting, May 2014

Address requests for information to:
SHEPHERD'S VOICE PUBLICATIONS, INC.
#60 Chicago St., Cubao, Quezon City, Philippines 1109
P.O. Box 1331 Quezon City Central Post Office
1153 Quezon City
Tel. No. (632) 725-9999, 725-1115, 725-1190, 411-7874
Fax. No. (632) 727-5615, 726-9918
E-mail: sales@shepherdsvoice.com.ph

Layout and design by Rey de Guzman

Table of Contents

Introduction

There's a Goliath in Your Life

He's big, tall and hairy.

With burly arms and a javelin the size of a missile. His shield is like a tank. His legs are like tree trunks.

One look at him and you freeze in terror. The monster is exceedingly arrogant and menacing in every way.

I don't know who or what your Goliath is.

Perhaps your Goliath is your financial problem.

Perhaps it's sickness.

Perhaps it's a difficult relationship.

Perhaps it's your boss.

Perhaps it's your mother-in-law.

Perhaps it's your personal weakness.

If you picked up this book just because you thought it has a nice cover or just because someone gave it to you then take it as a gift from heaven. A divine appointment, if you may.

Believe that God is giving you a message today. He's saying to you, "Kid, you may be small on the outside but you're big on the inside. You can conquer your Goliath. Because I created you and, as a policy, I only make champions. Nothing less."

This simple book with its simple words will seize you,

lift you up and encourage you. Its contents can change the
entire direction of your life. It can re-tool you to victory
and give you outrageous success in every area of your life,
more than you've ever dreamed of.

Get ready to win big time.

May your dreams come true,

Bo Sanchez

Bo Sanchez

P.S. **Get a unique, inspiring, powerful, personalized**
message from God each day. It'll blow you away.
Sign up at **www.GodWhispersClub.com** now!

What follows next is a creative rendition
of the ancient story of David and Goliath.
I must warn you that I inserted imaginative details
that aren't found in the original story.
Just read 1 Samuel 17 to get the real deal.
Mine is a Picasso version.
It's an abstract retelling of a tale that happened 3,000 years ago,
but whose power remains alive in our lives today.
Enjoy.

Book One

The Pebble That Crushed the Mountain

A group of kids were crowding around an old man.

"Uncle Kenjo! Is it true that you were in the Bible?"

"Who told you?" the grey-haired man asked in mock surprise.

The kids screamed, "King David! We met him yesterday!"

The old man laughed, "Awesome, isn't he?"

"Oh, yes!" the little ones cried out.

One girl said, "I like his singing voice so much. It's so peaceful, he puts me to sleep."

Everyone laughed.

"You should hear him play his harp, too," Kenjo said. "But tell me, now that you've met the real McCoy, why bother with me? I'm just a bit player."

The little girl said, "Because he was busy chatting with Prophet Elijah. He also said that you're one of the best storytellers ever. So can you tell us a Bible story? Pretty please?"

The old man couldn't resist.

He sat down and gathered the children. An entire afternoon gone, he thought. But he always loved sharing his days on earth. It had been thousands of years since but he still recalled them like they had happened last week.

A little boy climbed on his lap and said, "So, Uncle Kenjo, were you really in the Bible?"

"Well, my name was never mentioned. But yes, I was right there in the most famous fight in the Bible."

"Whoa. You mean the one between David and…?"

"Yep, big, bad boy Goliath himself. I saw it all. The slingshot, the javelin, the sword and the blood splattering on the desert sand."

"Way cooooool," the little kid said, his eyes popping. The kids sat around him in a tight circle. They knew they were in for a real treat.

Kenjo took a deep breath and began his story…

The Beginning

I started as King Saul's armor bearer.

I remember how thrilled Mama was when she heard my job title. She was so excited, she threw a little party in our town. She told all my relatives of my good fortune.

The next day, everyone in our town came to borrow money.

Well, don't be too impressed.

Yes, the pay was good, I got to stay in the palace and I saw VIPs every day. I also got to see all the beautiful girls in the palace. One of them eventually became my wife. We had four boys who all looked just like me. (I pitied them.)

But in reality, a royal armor bearer was a fancy name for the King's maid. A maid who just happened to be a guy. That's all.

Most of my days, you'd have found me cleaning and polishing the King's armor.

Scrub, scrub, scrub. That's what I did most days.

But because of the Philistine problem, the King used his armor a lot during those years.

The Philistines were our worst enemy.

I remember how I used to curse them.

Those morons (pardon my French) thought they could just swoop down on us, take our land, steal our women and make us slaves forever. What were these guys thinking? Didn't their mothers teach them good manners and right conduct?

I wondered if they actually had no mothers.

Well, one fateful day, these motherless creatures had a new leader. It was the big, bad boy himself, Mr. Goliath, and boy, oh boy, was the guy a walking freak show. He was a beast! He was Godzilla in disguise.

Frankly, I didn't think he was human.

In fact, among King Saul's soldiers, they called him The Mountain. Because his mere shadow covered two battalions.

I knew the army shouldn't be talking about how fearsome the beast was because it lowered their morale and all, but hey, I couldn't blame them. Goliath was just plain awesome.

And you should have heard him speak.

Two Spectacular Shows a Day

This is what happened.

Imagine this scene with me.

Two armies facing each other. The Israelites on one hill; the Philistines on the other. A valley in between them, also called No Man's Land.

The tension hanging in the air was exceedingly heavy.

All of a sudden, The Mountain, Godzilla, King Kong or whatever you want to call that beast, marched forward from the ranks of the Philistines. He was so humongous, it was as though the earth shook with every step he took. And in front of us — all 40,000 soldiers of King Saul — he screamed, "Who wants to challenge me to a duel? Choose one man from among you. If he kills me, all of us shall serve you. But if I kill him, you shall serve us!"

Can you imagine the effect this had on every single poor soldier of King Saul? They were gripped with terror!

Even his grizzled generals couldn't look directly at the King's eyes, lest he ask them, "Hey, why don't you go? You have life insurance, right?"

Do you know how often Goliath gave this speech? He gave this for 40 days straight. And he gave it twice a day. Like there was a matinee and a gala show. That was how popular it was. In fact, people lined up and watched it over and over again.

He was *that* good.

The Reward

So what did my boss do?

King Saul proclaimed a bounty for the head of Goliath.

It was a genius plan.

Except for one thing: It didn't work.

I was in the room when he announced it.

Saul declared, "Anyone who can give me Goliath's head on a platter, I shall make him a rich man. And I shall exempt him and his family from paying taxes for his entire lifetime. And I shall give him my daughter's hand in marriage."

Man, you could hear a pin drop.

It was clear that no one in the room was interested.

I elbowed my cousin, Goob, who was right beside me. He worked as a King's guard. I said, "Cuz, why don't you volunteer? You'll marry a princess!"

He elbowed me back and whispered, "The princess is cute but I have no desire to die early."

King Saul thought the reward was going to boost people's hopes. But it had the opposite effect. Now, everyone knew that the situation was desperate.

The news spread among the ranks of Saul's army, but the early gossip that the Palace received wasn't encouraging. The most common answer to the message about the reward was, "Sorry, I'm not cuckoo."

The Errand Boy Walks into the Scene

As the entire army of King Saul was turning to mush, out of the blue, a little pebble entered the scene.

His name was David.

Just to brag a bit, David was my boyhood chum. We actually played together as kids.

OK, I'm stretching it a bit.

Actually, I just played with him once. Some years back, my family visited his town. Much later, I told him this story and he said that he didn't remember my name at all.

But I remembered his — the name his friends called him.

It was Pebble.

Of course, David was bigger than a pebble.

But not that much.

If you compared him to his eight brothers (his eldest brother, Eliab, was even called "The Rock"), it was obvious how he got his pet name.

Most of his brothers were in the army, wearing brass helmets, heavy breastplates and long spears. David was a scrawny shepherd who walked into the scene carrying a basket. A basket, for crying out loud! If it weren't true, it would be funny.

David was there because his Mama had asked him to bring lunch to his brothers. Yep, our hero was an errand boy.

Focused on the Princess

That was when David saw Goliath. And I'm pretty sure he was scared like everyone else.

But people who witnessed this event told me that a strange thing happened when David heard about the King's reward. It was like the reward seized him, they said.

At that precise moment, everything changed. His attitude, his disposition, his posture. He stood taller. He spoke faster. Even his face changed. From fear, they could now only see passion. It was like his eyes were lit with fire.

And he kept asking again and again, "Tell me what will happen to the guy who defeats Goliath one more time, please?"

So the soldiers would tell him again.

"Tell me if I got this right," he asked, looking at his notes, "the man who defeats the giant, the King will reward with great riches, tax exemption and a beautiful princess. Am I right?"

That was when his brother, Eliab the Rock, saw him. He screamed, "Hey, Runt! Rodent!" He spat on the ground in disgust. "What do you think you are doing here? This is a for-adults-only party. Get back to your sheep, you insect!"

I wasn't there, but according to those who were, David wasn't upset at all. He was too focused! He simply said to Eliab, "Hey, bro, what's wrong? I'm just asking," and he turned around and continued talking with the soldiers and writing down his notes.

He asked, "How much riches are really involved here? Does it include gold and land? Do you think this includes cattle?"

On and on, the questions went. He asked, "Is the tax exemption total? VAT included? And did the King name the princess? Or will the guy be able to choose the princess he wants to marry?"

Finally, after he had heard enough, David shouted out for everyone to hear the line that made him the most famous warrior in the entire history of Israel. He said, "Who is this uncircumcised Philistine, that he should defy the armies of the living God?"

Quickly, the rumor spread through the ranks. A challenger has arisen! We now have someone insane enough to fight Goliath!

In minutes, King Saul was advised.
And he summoned David to his tent.
I remember that day very well.
I was there. I saw it all.

Let Me Do It My Way

In the midst of the generals and officers around the King, little David walked in. The contrast couldn't have been more shocking.

The generals were burly and muscular, their bodies covered with steel and leather. David was thin and young, wearing his woollen shepherd's shirt that had seen better days. I could smell him from 10 feet away. Goodness, he was even barefoot.

You could see the disappointment in everyone's faces. His appearance dashed their hopes to the ground. They had no challenger for Goliath after all. One of the King's officials near me said, "He's probably a nutcase. This is a waste of time."

King Saul voiced everyone's thoughts. "How could I send you to fight Goliath? You're just a kid."

That was when David spoke with such power, it rocked the room. I don't mean he shouted. It's just the way he said it.

He said, "Yes, I'm a kid. But I'm also a shepherd who protected my sheep by fighting bears and lions — and I killed them."

The room buzzed with grown-up men arguing like kids fighting in the playground.

David continued, "And this giant will fall in the same way!"

The buzz grew louder.

The King silenced everyone with a wave of his hand. He said, "If you will fight Goliath, you'll need equipment." He snapped his fingers.

That was where I, Kenjo, entered the story.

I stepped forward, carrying the royal armor.

"Put it on him," the King ordered me.

David removed his woolen shirt and stretched out his arms.

My golly gee, was the guy thin!

You could see his rib cage sticking out.

I put on the heavy breastplate on his scrawny chest. It almost reached his knees.

I strapped the belt around his waist. I had to loop it around a number of times.

I clamped the shoulder pads, tied the sandals on his dirty feet and handed him the royal shield and the royal sword.

I looked at him. David didn't look like a warrior. He looked like a Christmas tree.

And David knew it, too.

He said, "King, I'm touched that you're lending me your armor, but this isn't me. I'm just not used to it. If I wear this, I won't be able to kill Goliath."

David removed the armor pieces one by one. He smiled at me and said, "Thanks. Perhaps on another day, when I'm older."

I nodded.

I didn't know that his words were prophetic.

As I was packing the armor back in its storage place, David had already run out of the tent to face the monster.

The Duel

Along the way, David picked up five smooth stones. That was all he needed. Nothing else.

It was now time.

He marched towards the Philistine army.

As he came nearer, David shouted a challenge to his enemy that was downright spine-tingling. Every hair on my body stood on end.

He said, *"You come to me with a sword and with a spear and with a javelin; but I come to you in the name of the Lord of hosts, the God of the armies of Israel, whom you have defied.... This day the Lord will deliver you into my hand, and I will strike you down, and cut off your head; and I will give the dead bodies of the host of the Philistines this day to the birds of the air and to the wild beasts of the earth... and that all this assembly may know that the Lord saves not with sword and spear; for the battle is the Lord's and he will give you into our hand."*

Big words. But half of me wondered if they were just empty words. From the hill, King Saul and all his 40,000 soldiers were watching, hearts pounding in their chest.

That was when Goliath came forward, like a wild beast bursting from its cage.

A Pebble against a Mountain!

Soon, we heard Goliath's fiendish laughter. "Doesn't Saul have better soldiers than this mouse?"

I glanced at the face of the King.

If he felt shame for his decision, he was hiding it well.

But I overheard one of the generals say to those around him, "I knew we shouldn't have sent that twirp. This is a very big mistake. We'll be the laughing stock of the world."

Suddenly, Goliath threw his spear at David.

The mighty weapon sliced through the air. David jumped and the missile zipped past him, missing his shoulder by an inch.

That was when David placed one smooth stone in his leather sling. And he started running towards the giant.

Whacked!

Now I think that was — and still is — the most magical sight I had ever seen. David running *towards* Goliath. Man! I wish I had captured it on film so I could show it to my kids and grandkids again and again.

I bet Goliath never saw that before either. He was used to entire battalions running away from him.

As expected, Goliath stood his ground — laughing like a mad man.

David, while running at breakneck speed, was still spinning his weapon of choice above his head. And some 12 meters from Goliath, he flung it. He flung it with all his might. He flung it like it was the last thing he would do on earth.

One stone. One forehead. Thud.

We didn't even hear the "thud" from where we stood.

We just saw the giant's body fall to the ground like a log.

A Pebble had crushed The Mountain!

And David, still running, reached for the enormous sword of Goliath. The sword was bigger than him. But he carried it like it was just a stick. It was adrenalin, people would later say.

And David sliced the giant's head off. Whack!

Instantly, the crowd around me exploded in a roar so loud I sometimes still feel it in my ears to this day.

That was 3,000 years ago.

A Message to Be Sent to the World

"Wow."

That was the only thing the kids could say.

Their eyes were still fixed on their storyteller, completely mesmerized.

Kenjo asked, "By the way, kids, how's the training?"

"Huh? Oh, the Angel Training!" said one boy, "We're doing OK, Uncle Kenjo. This is part of our training — interviewing the guys from the Bible. So far, it's been an amazing ride."

The man smiled, "And when will you be sent to Earth?"

"Oh, perhaps in a few more years we'll see some action."

He nodded. "Hey, little angels, can you do me a favor?"

"Sure thing," they said.

"Years after the David and Goliath fight, did you know that I became King David's armor bearer?"

"Wow," one of them said.

"Let me continue my story. After defeating Goliath, King David saw lots of battles in his life. And I stood beside him, watching him win again and again on the battlefield. He won so often, it got boring.

"But none of those victories compared with the first one. The one with the big, bad boy, Goliath.

"In fact, in my private conversations with King David, he told me why he won every battle. He said he learned crucial lessons from conquering the Philistine giant.

"Every time we chatted, he shared one lesson. Through the years, I wrote them down. He told me, 'Kenjo, if you want to conquer your Goliath, learn these lessons well.'

"While I lived on earth, they were the lessons that blessed my human life so much.

"Do you want to know what they are?"

The little angels around him said, "Yes!"

Kenjo pulled out a slip of paper from his pocket.

He said, "Here they are."

On the simple piece of paper, it said…

7 Keys of a Champion's Life
1. Follow Your Dream with Passion
2. Focus on Your Core Gift
3. Believe in Yourself When Others Don't
4. Build Your Team
5. Take Action
6. Fail Forward
7. Shine Your Light

One little angel asked, "You said you were going to ask a favor, Uncle Kenjo."

The old man smiled, rolled up the piece of paper and handed it to the little one. "When you go down to Planet Earth, share these lessons to people who are facing big problems in life."

"As big as Goliath?" the little angel asked.

"Yes, as big as Goliath. Tell them they can win. If tiny David can win, anyone can."

All the little angels hugged the old man. "Thanks for the story, Uncle Kenjo. And don't worry. We'll spread these words."

"Thank you," the older man replied, "Thank you very much."

Why You're Holding This Book Today

Fast-forward to a few years later. Those little angels grew up and were finally sent to Earth.

Perhaps when I was facing my biggest problems and I was alone wondering what I should do with my life, one of those angels whispered these thoughts to my heart.

Who knows?

All I know is that these powerful principles have blessed my life so much.

And I'd like to share them with you.

Happy reading.

Book Two

7 Keys of a Champion's Life

Key #1

Follow Your Dream
with Passion

*Know What You Want
and Pursue It*

*If you are bored with life, if you don't get up every morning with
a burning desire to do things — you don't have enough goals.*
— Lou Holtz

Chapter 1

Find Something You're Willing to Die For

It was the first time I visited Las Vegas.

The sights were overwhelming.

The lights, the hotels, the fountains and the casinos — it was all an incredible sight.

On the way to a restaurant, I remember walking through endless rows of slot machines. I saw the players — mostly old people — sitting in front of the machines.

I wondered: How long have they been here?

Even as fast music and blinking lights surrounded them, I sensed sadness in some of them.

After our meal, my friends and I went to watch a concert in a theater on the upper floor of that gigantic hotel.

After the two-hour show, I had to pass through the lobby with the slot machines again.

And there they were, the same people playing the machines!

I noticed one man.

Medium-built. In his 50s. Tired. He seemed so miserable doing what he was doing.

I looked at his eyes.

Call it discernment. Call it just a wild hunch. Call it whatever you want. But I felt there was so much emptiness in his life.

It was like he woke up every morning not knowing what to do. So he comes here just to spend his money and time on nothing.

Seeing him broke my heart.

I wanted to pull him out and tell him, "Do you want real joy? This isn't the place. Come with me to the Philippines. So many poor people have no homes. You can help us build homes for them. So many poor kids are begging on the streets. You can send them to school. Perhaps you'll find your purpose there."

I walked out of the hotel feeling foolish for thinking this way.

But I really believe that unless a person finds a purpose bigger than himself, life will always be empty.

Friend, have you found yours?

Have you a found a dream worthy enough that you're willing to die for it?

Self-Oriented Dreams Are OK as Long as They're Not Purely Self-Oriented

I believe a person without dreams is like a zombie.

He's still breathing and walking and working, but a part of him is already dead. Because he just goes through the motions of living.

Search your heart.

What are your dreams?

Perhaps your dream is to have your own house.

Or to drive a new car.

Or to send all your kids to school.

Or to build your own business.

Or to become vice president of a company.

Or to travel around the world.

Some extremely religious people look down on these dreams. Because they're still self-oriented.

They only praise "holy" dreams like building an orphanage, or evangelizing the lost, or becoming a missionary, or sending poor kids to school, or building a microlending program in slum areas.

But I disagree.

You can't judge people by the dream itself.

A person who dreams of building an orphanage may be doing it for his own glory, while a person who dreams of a new car may want it to serve his family and friends.

There's nothing wrong with self-oriented dreams — as long as they're not *purely* self-oriented.

I believe that God plants dreams in our hearts. And these dreams will always be — ultimately — a blessing for others. This is the only way to real happiness.

God made you for a purpose bigger than yourself.

Your dreams may bless you first — but that's so you can be a rich blessing to others.

Like David's dream.

It's OK If a Dream Isn't for God Alone

The statement above sounds heretical, but it's not.

In fighting Goliath, David was willing to die for God. That was clear in the biblical text. He loved God.

But the Bible specifically says that David also did it for himself. David fought Goliath because he liked the reward. He did it for his family's well-being, too. And I don't think there's anything wrong with that.

It doesn't make him less spiritual.

For example, some of my religious friends didn't understand why I got into business some years ago. A few of them were disappointed. They said that because I was their preacher, they wanted me to remain pure, untouched by the world.

But I wasn't celibate. I had a family to feed. And because I was in ministry, I also had a long line of people that kept asking me for help — and I didn't have any means to help them.

A few people think there's something wrong with doing something for yourself. That somehow, it lessens your brownie points in heaven. Some people believe that you should do everything for God *alone* and not mix it with anything that is self-rewarding.

Question: Why can't I do things for *both* God and me? I love me! And God loves me, too!

Frankly, I do it all the time: I love God and me at the same time.

And I'm sure you do it all the time, too.

For example, I eat because I'm hungry. That's self-oriented. But I eat also because I want to serve God with a healthy body. (But I must confess that the second cup of ice cream I ate last night wasn't very healthy. Sorry, Lord.)

I brush my teeth daily so I can eat well and remain *guwapo*[1] when I smile. That's self-oriented. But I also do it because I don't want people around me to be victims of chemical warfare.

---

[1] handsome

I earn money so I can buy my favorite peanut butter, feed my kids, date my wife each week and go on family vacations. That's sort of self-oriented. But I also do it because I want to feed poor kids and fund the work of the Kingdom.

The key is to not *just* do it for yourself.

Or your heart will never be at peace.

Yes, a dream must be bigger than yourself.

There will be a throbbing emptiness within you that you can't quiet unless you love more than just yourself.

Loving yourself is just the beginning.

You need to dream bigger dreams!

Note: Years ago, I published an e-book entitled *How to Know If Your Dreams Are God's Dreams.* You can download it for free from my website, **www.BoSanchez.ph.** It will help you discern which dreams you should pursue.

Chapter 2

Focus on the Dream, Not the Giant

I don't understand mean jokes about mothers-in-law.
I love my mother-in-law.
She's a jewel, one of God's best gifts to me.

Personally, I have a suspicion that she loves me now more than she does her daughter, but that's just our little secret. Don't tell my wife.

For 20 years, my mother-in-law worked for a company that sold educational plans, pension plans and other financial products. For obvious reasons, I bought various plans from her. Through the many years, my investments accumulated to P900,000 and I dreamt of getting a nice sum when the plans matured.

But one day, I read in the newspaper that her company was failing. In a snap, I saw my investments disappear.

My mother-in-law didn't know what had happened either. Being in the sales department, she was completely in the dark, too. She was so embarrassed and apologized to me profusely. I told her, "Mommy, it's OK. That's just money. I'll earn it back." (I also told her, "I didn't lose anything." I placed my arm around her daughter and said, "I've got my real wealth right here beside me.")

When I experience trials, I try to follow this powerful principle: *Focus on the dream, not the giant.*

Whenever I have a problem, I never waste my time or energy focusing on the problem. I'd rather spend my time and energy on my dream. My dream of investing in her company was to make lots of money. If her company failed, that doesn't mean my dream failed with it. I will still fulfill my dream. I will earn that money.

Focusing on your problem depresses your spirit.[2] It limits your vision. It traps you into a hole.

Focusing on your dream is different. It energizes you. It expands your vision. You see new opportunities you never saw before.

Instead of regaining back P900,000 from the failed company, I chose to earn 10 times that amount in other ways. Today, I've fulfilled that goal. Because of this, I was able to give so much more to the ministry.

Imagine the other scenario. Let's say I focused my work on getting the P900,000 back from that company. And let's say I actually got it back. (Fat chance but suspend analytical thinking.) Aside from the worry and anger I would have accumulated in my heart, I would have gotten P900,000 only.

Don't Make the Mistake of Watching the Problem for 40 Days and Nights

Saul's army chose to listen to Goliath's speech for 40 days and nights. They focused on the giant.

Soldier 1: "My gosh, look at those biceps."

Soldier 2: "It's as big as my torso."

Soldier 1: "Do you think he eats people?"

---

[2] Proverbs 17:22 "A joyful heart is the health of the body, but a depressed spirit dries up the bones."

Soldier 2: "I wouldn't be surprised if he was a cannibal. He seems to have fangs. Perhaps he's also a vampire."

Soldier 1: "I don't know. Maybe he's an alien. Inside that human skin, he's really an 80-foot scaly lizard."

Soldier 2: "You think he'll speak again tomorrow? I'll tell my neighbors to come and watch this."

Soldier 1: "Tell them to come early if they want to get good seats. I'll bring some popcorn."

Soldier 2: "Cool. I'll bring the drinks."

David didn't do any of that.

Instead, he focused on the reward.

He focused on the dream.

He focused on the princess.

And that's what you need to do, too.

Hey, if you experience a loss, it's OK to cry. To grieve. To acknowledge the hurt. To mourn the loss.

We need that.

Because grief heals.

But grief, if extended far too long, will kill.[3]

Get up.

Find your dream.

Find your passion.

And pursue it.

---

[3] Proverbs 18:14 (NLT) "The human spirit can endure a sick body, but who can bear a crushed spirit?"

Chapter 3

Repeat the Dream to Yourself Again and Again

David wanted to hear about the reward again and again.

Champions are like that.

From experience, champions write their dreams down. And champions read them often, pray about them often and visualize them often.

I share about this great study all the time: In 1957, Harvard University asked their graduates whether they write down their dreams. Only 3 percent of the entire batch answered yes. Twenty years later, in 1977, they went back to these same graduates and what the researchers found out astounded them. The assets of the 3 percent who wrote down their goals outweighed the assets of the 97 percent combined.

One night in 1997, I wrote my dreams.

I nicknamed it my *Dream Book* and it was 15 pages long.

Let me now give you one of the most powerful success habits of my life. Since that fateful night in 1997, I've *read* my Life Dreams every day. No kidding.

Each morning, as part of my prayer, I read my dreams and present them to God. I declare it anew to myself, to the world, to the universe. I remind myself of my future.

It's so powerful, I wake up each morning knowing exactly what I want to do with my life.

So writing down your dreams is fantastic. By itself, it already unlocks the blessings of the universe upon your life. By writing down your dreams, you open yourself to life's river of abundance.

But when you read your dreams every day, you multiply the power of that river tenfold.

If you don't like reading them, hang photos of your dreams on your bedroom wall. Look at them every day. Pray for them every day.

Chapter 4

Make Your Dream as Graphic as You Can

When David spoke to Goliath, he was very graphic.

He said, "This day the Lord will deliver you into my hand, and I will strike you down, and cut off your head; and I will give the dead bodies of the host of the Philistines this day to the birds of the air and to the wild beasts of the earth."

I know, it's gory, but I'm driving home a point: Your dream should be graphic.

Graphic details trigger your emotions.

They give you energy — something you need when you want to conquer Goliaths and achieve your dreams.

If it's going to be graphic, you'll need imagination.

That's why the great Albert Einstein said, "Imagination is everything. It is the preview of life's coming attractions."

It's also why Olympic champions visualize their goals. Coaches tell their athletes to win first in their minds if they want to win in the field.

So a runner imagines himself crossing the finish line.

A gymnast imagines herself doing the perfect floor routine.

A basketball player imagines himself making many three-point shots.

Champion athletes visualize *constantly*.

In the same way, champions in life create visions of their desired future in their minds.

Graphic Means Specific

In the last chapter, I mentioned that my Dream Book is 15 pages long. Why so many pages? Because my dreams are clothed with color, texture, sizes, shapes, tastes, smells and sounds.

The more specific, the better.

Is your dream to lose weight?

Don't say, "I want to lose weight."

That's too blah. And when it comes to dreams, being unimaginative is a crime. Speak from the heart. What do you really want?

Instead of saying, "I want to lose weight," say instead, "I weigh 120 pounds by December 31, 2017. My children look at me and say, 'Wow, you did it, Mom!' I'll buy a whole new wardrobe because all my clothes are too big. I can walk long distances and not feel tired at all. I feel healthy, strong and full of energy every day."

Don't just say, "I want to earn more money." Say instead, "I earn P120,000 a month by December 2017. I'll be able to pay the tuition fees of my kids on time, bring out my wife on a weekly date and give 12 percent of my income to God."

Don't just say, "I want to have my own house." Say instead, "I own a two-bedroom condo in Makati by December

2017. It's a beautiful home filled with love, noisy meals with my kids and friendly neighbors around me."

Success author Napoleon Hill said, "Whatever the mind can conceive and believe, it can achieve." Let me change his words a bit: Whatever the mind can *imagine* and believe, it can achieve.

Note: I give away a simple tool to write your dreams. I call it the *Life Dreams and Success Journal*. We give it as a gift to all those who support our ministries. Log on to **www. KerygmaFamily.com** now.

Key #2

Focus on Your Core Gift

Use Your Strength, Not Your Weakness

Success follows doing what you want to do.
There is no other way to be successful.
— Malcolm Forbes

Chapter 5

Discover Your Core Gift

David was given a King's sword.

I'm sure it was the most expensive in the land.

I bet it was made of the finest materials money could buy, made by the best craftsman in the entire country.

Yet when David held it in his hand, his heart knew it wasn't going to fulfill his dream. It may have been the best weapon in the land, but it wasn't the best weapon for him. Because he knew that his core gift wasn't to wield a sword, but to fling a slingshot.

How did he know?

Many times, he was able to kill bears and lions with targeted stones speeding at killer velocities.

Friend, let me ask you: *What is your slingshot?*

The only way you can defeat your Goliath is to stick to your core gift. The more you know your core gift, the more successful you become. The less you know what your core gift is, the less successful you will be. Find your core gift, use it and you will bless the world.

Here's how you'll know your core gift.

First, check out your *trail of blessings.* David looked back and saw that God blessed him whenever he used the slingshot. He enjoyed much success when he used it.

First, Look for Your "Trail of Blessings"

Where has God been blessing you in the past?

That's more likely where God will continue to bless you.

For the past 30 years, I've been preaching and writing with great success. I don't expect God to suddenly use me as a dance choreographer, computer programmer or a gourmet chef.

You simply have to follow the trail of blessings in your life.

I've realized this even in entrepreneurship.

When I start a business that's not in line with my core gift, which is my communication skills, I lose a lot of money. There's a learning curve that I have to go through before that business gets profitable.

But if I start a business that uses communication skills, there's no learning curve. I earn money almost immediately after I start it.

Let me ask you this question: *What have you done in your life that has had the greatest impact on people's lives?*

Many people are stuck because they don't know their slingshot. Other people are stuck because they know their slingshot, but they're not using it.

Are you stuck now with a sword and not a slingshot?

Make the switch.

Be faithful to your core gift, whatever it is.

For some of you, it's technology.

For some of you, it's giving financial wisdom.

For some of you, it's accounting.

For some of you, it's working with your hands.

For some of you, it's your people skills.

For some of you, it's teaching the next generation.

For some of you, it's preaching.

For some of you, it's raising your kids as a full-time mother.

For some of you, it's selling products that will bless people.

Be faithful to your core gift and you'll be successful.

Second, Follow Your Passion

In other words, do what you *love to do*.

The happiest people I know are those who have discovered their passion — and work within the circle of their passion.

The great Michelangelo created incredible works, from David, The Dying Slave, The Laurentian Library, the entire ceiling of the Sistine Chapel and The Pieta in St. Peter's Cathedral.

Why so prolific? He just loved doing it. He would do it even if he didn't get paid.

People ask me, "Why are you so prolific, Bo? Why are you able to write three to four books a year?"

Because writing is my passion. I just love to write!

Because of this, I have no time for writer's block.

Here's the last thing you need to do.

Third, Match Your Core Gift to Your Market

It's not enough to know your core gift. You need to know how your core gift can meet a felt need in your target market.

In creating your product, you still have to check what your customers want. In other words, your product must be market driven.

For example, I can write seriously. Boring, dry, textbook style writing. But I choose to write with humor.

Why? Because I write to Filipinos and Filipinos love to laugh, even when the topic is serious.

I've long learned that if you want to have a large readership in the Philippines, you need to write with humor. (Would you believe that the top selling books in the Philippines are joke books?)

Chapter 6

Develop Your Core Gift

The best way to develop your core gift is to use it.
Again and again and again.

The second best way to develop your core gift is to get trained. Make your strength even stronger — because that's your special gift to the world.

Do people tell you that you're a good cook?

Don't stop cooking. Don't stop experimenting. Don't stop studying, attending cooking seminars and talking with chefs from different cities. Develop your craft!

Author Richard Koch says, "Everyone can achieve something significant. The key is not effort but finding the right thing to achieve. You are hugely more productive at some things than at others but you dilute the effectiveness of this by doing too many things where your comparative skill is nowhere as great."

Recently, I bought P20,000 worth of audio CDs to improve my communication skills. When I told my friend about it, he was stunned. He asked me, "How long have you been preaching, Bo?"

I said, "Thirty years."

He shook his head, "And you're still studying how to communicate? You're crazy!"

I am. I'm crazy about developing my craft.

Every year, I spend more than P150,000 on books just to grow in wisdom. I read all sorts of books — spiritual books, financial books, human development books. Why? I can't give what I don't have. I need to keep on growing so I could help others keep growing, too. It's part of my job.

I have so many books, my wife tells me that our house no longer has a library. Our library has a house.

Friend, be totally committed to developing your core gift.

Chapter 7

Delegate Your Weakness

David delegated his weakness.

He knew his weakness was the sword.

He knew he was no match for Goliath if they would have a sword fight. So he stayed in his area of strength — he used his slingshot.

But read carefully: He delegated to Goliath the task of carrying a sword. When he needed it, he simply took the giant's sword — and killed him with it.

At the start of anything — a business, an organization, a project — you may have to do everything. But pretty soon, you will have to focus on your strength and delegate your weakness to others.

I like what German playwright Johann Wolfang von Goethe said. "Things that matter most must never be at the mercy of things that matter least."

Economist Vilfredo Pareto was the one who came up with the 80/20 Principle. Quality guru Joseph Juran called it the "Rule of the Vital Few." Here's what it means: *80 percent of results come from only 20 percent of inputs.* Always remember that when you use your core gifts, that's the 20 percent input that will produce 80 percent of the results.

In my ministries, I don't take care of the accounting. I don't make my websites. I don't take care of administration work. I just focus on preaching and leadership. That may be 20 percent of the organization but that takes care of 80 percent of its results.

It Applies to Business

I started Shepherd's Voice Publications 20 years ago.

At the beginning, I did everything: I wrote the entire magazine, chose the fonts, designed cover concepts and even drew all the illustrations. I also took out the trash, answered the phones and marketed the magazine.

Today, I just write. Because of this laser-like focus, we grew. We now publish eight periodicals and a slew of books, produce CDs and DVDs, TV shows, SMS content, radio programs and Internet sites — anything that can communicate God's love.

I'll give you an example of how ruthless you should be when it comes to focusing on your strength and delegating your weakness.

For the longest time, people asked me, "Bo, do you have a printing press?"

People get shocked when I tell them we don't have any. "What? You publish so much material. Won't you save money if you had your own printing machines?"

Perhaps we would. But you see, it'll take my focus away from what I do best — writing. Running a printing press, maintaining the machines and hiring the people who run them are not my expertise. So I'd rather focus on one thing — writing — and delegate everything else to other companies.

Here's the key to success: Do what you do best and ask others to do what they do best.

It Applies to Your Personal Talents

I was born in Manila. But when I was one year old, my father's company assigned him to Cebu. We lived on that island for seven years.

Because of that short stint, I failed to learn Tagalog. When I got back to Manila, I only spoke English.

Bad for me. I kept flunking Filipino in school.

By age 13, I was preaching. And I preached in pure English.

But I had a great love for the poor and I dreamt of reaching out to them. But I just couldn't preach in Tagalog.

I lived in Anawim for three years, our ministry for the abandoned elderly. I remember coming home from Canada. I preached to 800 plus Canadians without a sweat. When I arrived in Anawim, I led the prayer meeting of 20 old people. I fumbled so much with my Tagalog, I couldn't connect with them. It was so frustrating.

Here's what I realized: My gift is preaching and writing in English is my strength. Whenever I preach to a middle class crowd, I flourish. People come in droves. When I preach to a Tagalog-speaking crowd, I'm OK. But not great.

There is a niche for me out there — people who need to hear God's Word in English.

Your core gift has a corresponding market niche.

When you identify your core gift, you identify your boundaries.

The clearer your boundaries, the more successful you become.

Define your audience now.

When David marched towards Goliath with a slingshot, his enemies laughed. When you march towards your market with your core gift, people may ridicule you.

That's OK.

Do it anyway.

Your success won't be far away.

Key #3

Believe in Yourself When Others Don't

Here's the Truth: God Believes in You!

Sooner or later, those who win are those who think they can.
—Richard Bach,
Jonathan Livingston Seagull

Chapter 8

Build Your Confidence by Starting Small

David didn't have false humility.

When he presented himself to King Saul, he said, "Your servant has killed both lions and bears; and this uncircumcised Philistine shall be like one of them..."[4]

David believed in himself and his core ability to perform.

If you don't believe in you, who will?

If you don't have this confidence, I have a recommendation for you: *Start small.*

David began with bears and lions before he fought Goliath.

Imagine if he hadn't started small...

David: "Hi, King Saul, I'm the Giant Slayer at your service. I'm here to take care of this pest that's been bothering you lately."

King Saul: "Uh-huh. Any previous experience of killing giants?"

David: "None whatsoever. But I did kill mosquitoes. Just not the fat ones that have sucked a meal already. Splattered blood makes me queasy."

---
[4] 1 Samuel 17:36

King Saul: "I see. So what makes you think you can kill Goliath?"

David: "I just have this feeling."

King Saul: "Feeling?"

David: "Yes. A feeling. I'm very excited."

King Saul: "Wow, that's wonderful." (He then faces his guards.) "My dear soldiers, can you escort this young gentlemen to our pet tigers? I think it's lunchtime."

Before Big Deals, Start with Small Deals

There's a pricey but excellent board game made by Robert Kiyosaki, author of *Rich Dad, Poor Dad*, called Cashflow. Instead of learning financial wisdom through lectures, you learn by playing a game. And one of the most important lessons you'll learn is to always start with "Small Deals" before you go to "Big Deals."

It's so obvious yet I see so many people do the very opposite.

They go for the Big Deals first, get burned and go make Small Deals later.

If you're putting up your first business, I suggest you don't put up a multinational corporation. Downscale it a bit.[5] How about a trading firm with one employee — you?

When I started preaching, I didn't speak at the Araneta Coliseum right away. I preached at our little prayer group of 20 people — composed of my mother, my five sisters, their husbands, my three aunts, five cousins, their boyfriends and two lazy cats.

As I grew in experience, I began to believe in the core gifts that God has given me.

---

[5] Mark 4:30-32 The Parable of the Mustard Seed

After three years, at age 16, I was ready for the coliseum.

Today, I've preached in Australia, New Zealand, Singapore, Hong Kong, Brunei, Guam, Saipan, Vietnam, Thailand, Malaysia, Indonesia, Dubai, Belgium, England, Switzerland, Scotland... and 37 cities in North America.

It's been an amazing journey.

But where did this journey begin?

A very biased group of 20 people and two cats.

Chapter 9

Don't Listen to Negative People

When Goliath saw David, he said, "What do you think of me, a dog that you'll drive away with stones and sticks?" And the Philistine cursed David by his gods.[6]

You know what? I don't think that hurt David at all.

Because it came from the enemy.

We expect enemies to curse us.

But from my experience, when family and friends put us down, that's when we get wounded. Because they're family and friends, our hearts are vulnerable. Their words can hurt us deeply.

Remember Eliab, the brother of David? Eliab even scolded him for being there. He basically told David, "Why have you come down? And with whom have you left those few sheep in the wilderness? I know your presumption, and the evil of your heart; for you have come down to see the battle."[7]

Eliab judged his brother's heart. He called him evil!

If you're pursuing your dream, brace yourself.

Some of the people closest to you won't believe in your dreams.

---

[6] 1 Samuel 17:43
[7] 1 Samuel 17:28

Some will ridicule you, insult you and call you names. Others, with very good intentions, will hold you back. Jesus suffered the same persecution from his family.[8]

I've noticed something that happens often: When a person has an ambition, some of his religious friends would judge him and say, "That's selfishness," or "That's greed," or "That's materialism."

Sometimes, this comes from envy and insecurity. They can't handle the fact that you're going somewhere and they're stuck.

Sometimes, however, these friends speak from genuine concern.

This was what happened to a young friend of mine…

Golden Handcuffs

I have this young friend whom I felt had a strong calling in his life.

I was very impressed by his preaching gifts. I told him so. But his inner character was even more impressive. It was clear to me that he could be a great full-time lay missionary.

So I offered him a job in one of our organizations. I offered him the same salary that he was getting from his secular job. I also told him to get into entrepreneurship even as he serves in ministry. (I believe that lay missionaries must know how to handle money so they can pastor people in their financial lives.)

When I invited him to work with me, his eyes sparkled with joy. He said it had always been his dream to go into full-time ministry. He said he'd pray hard about it.

---

[8] Mark 3:21

A month later, we met over coffee.

With much sadness, he told me, "I don't think I can make the switch now. But I'm sure I'll do it perhaps two or three years down the road — if your offer still stands."

I asked him why the change of heart.

He said, "I called up two very close friends about your invitation. Both of them panicked. They asked to meet with me right away. With much love for me, they told me to think about my future. They advised me not to give up the security of my huge company and the future of my career."

"I'll respect your decision," I told him, "because at the end of the day, you'll live with it."

"Thanks, Brother Bo. Anyway, I can still serve after office hours and during weekends."

"No problem," I told him, "we'll keep in touch."

In my mind, the image I had of my friend was a man with golden handcuffs around his wrists. Just because it's gold, he didn't want to take them off.

Each year, I waited.

My young friend still couldn't decide.

Seek Advice from People
Who Are Already Living Your Dream

Finally, after three years, he came up to me and said, "I'm ready." At last. He left his job, joined our organization and hit the road running.

A few months later, he came up to me and said, "Brother Bo, I've never been happier in my life. This is what I was made for — sharing God's love and making disciples every day." I sensed a beautiful joy in him.

He also shared with me an interesting thing: how he was earning more — because he now had time to build up his other income streams. Once he took off the golden handcuffs, he found more gold.

He told me, "I regret why I waited for three years to do this!"

It's the same story for many people. We allow well-meaning friends to talk us out of our dreams.

I think it's crazy to ask advice from people who aren't already living the dream you aspire for. Just because they're wise in one thing doesn't mean they're wise in all things. It's like asking the best CPA if you should have an appendectomy or not.

My young friend sought advice from people who worked in companies all their lives. He should have asked advice from those who were living his dream — full-time lay missionaries.

Let me give you other examples.

If your dream is to climb the corporate ladder, don't seek advice from entrepreneurs. They won't understand you. Seek advice from vice presidents.

If your dream is to become an entrepreneur, don't seek advice from employees. They won't understand you. Seek advice from successful entrepreneurs.

Surround yourself with people who are living your dream, whatever your dream is.

These people will inspire you and teach you. They will also be honest with you and tell if your core gifts lie elsewhere. They will also protect you from thieves of the dream.

Don't Give Up Your Dream Amidst Rejection

Colonel Sanders believed he had a great chicken recipe.

He went from one restaurant to another, selling his chicken recipe for a nickel for every dish sold. He was rejected 1,012 times! But he didn't stop. One restaurant finally bought it and Kentucky Fried Chicken was born.

Jack Canfield and Mark Hanson wrote a book. Like any other author, they went about searching for a publisher. They approached 33 publishers in New York and 90 publishers in California, but all of them said, "No, we're not interested."

Finally, a small publisher accepted it.

Those 33 publishers in New York and 90 publishers in California must be very sad every time they see *Chicken Soup for the Soul* in bookstores. The book they rejected has now sold over 53 million copies.

Friend, never give up on your dream.

Chapter 10

Go for Your Target Market

Champions don't try to please everyone.

By the very nature of their passion, champions will create enemies. If you don't receive criticism, you're not a champion.

Champions aren't afraid to do crazy things that will excite one audience and infuriate another.

Champions have identified their target market and focus on meeting their needs. To do this, they forget everyone else.

If someone is criticizing you, ask if he belongs to your target market. If not, don't listen to him.

By the way, this is very difficult for me to apply in my life.

In my book, *Your Past Does Not Define Your Future,* I talked about my raging approval addiction. I was a severe people pleaser. Every morning, I'd wake up feeling so ashamed of myself.

This was rooted in my being molested as a child.

I had a deeply wounded heart and I longed for love. To fill that gaping wound, I needed everyone to like me. I would bend over backwards and do everything so people would like me. If one person didn't like me, I panicked. I felt like I was going to die.

Through the years, God has healed me. But this weakness rears its ugly head every once in a while.

Like when a priest criticized my writing.

A Critic Not from Your Target Market?

One day, a priest came up to me and said, "Bo, I don't like your writing style. It's all stories! And usually, it's stories about you. You glorify yourself. Why don't you just give the pure, unadulterated Word of God in your writings?"

I said, "Thank you for your comments, Father."

His words hurt because he was right.

So let me make a confession: There are probably times when I write so that my readers will like me. Unconsciously and consciously, I'm sure it happens. Who doesn't want to be liked?

But let me also say this as strongly as I can: *I write because I love you.* I have a great desire to bless your life. My deepest joy is to see you receive the abundance of God.

So my motives are mixed. I'm a complex creature. Like every other human being in this world!

But here's a very important point.

There I was, wanting to please this man of God in clerical garb.

But immediately, I knew he wasn't my target market.

I never wrote for priests. Goodness, they have their theology textbooks. No need to write for them. (Though lots of priests write to me to tell me they love my books, too.)

This is my target market: I write for ordinary lay people. And lay people don't read heavy theology books. They like reading stories!

So I filtered the priest's criticism — picked up the gold and threw the rest in the trash.

Because a champion will always serve his target market.

Key #4

Build Your Dream Team

Your Real Wealth Isn't Your Money, But the People in Your Life

"God, grant me the senility to forget the people I never liked anyway, the good fortune to run into the ones I do, and the eyesight to tell the difference."
— Anonymous

Chapter 11

Build a Dream Team

I believe that life is a team sport.

When you build your career or business, you need a team of people who will support you. Specifically, you need (1) mentors, (2) peers, (3) assistants and (4) customers.

Many fail in their career or business because they don't have mentors.[9] Others fail because they picked the wrong peers and assistants. So instead of a Dream Team, they have a Nightmare Team. And others fail because they themselves are the nightmare. Because they can't work with others.

Too bad. In one landmark study, 1,000 CEOs in America were asked, "What is the most important quality you look for in an employee?" The results were a landslide. The #1 desired quality is the *ability to work with a wide range of people.*

Family Life Needs Team Effort

It takes a village to raise a child.

When you build a family, you need to assemble a Dream Team around you. Don't do it alone.

---

[9] Sirach 6:34-36 "Frequent the company of the elders; whoever is wise, stay close to him. Be eager to hear every godly discourse; let no wise saying escape you. If you see a man of prudence, seek him out; let your feet wear away his doorstep!"

Building a family is as important as and, in one sense, more important than building a multinational corporation. You need mentors, peers and assistants, too. To raise your kids, you need grandparents, siblings, neighbors, teachers, tutors, friends.... And I believe one of the great blessings of joining a spiritual community like ours is raising your kids within a culture that can build values in them. This is why I have so much passion to build my spiritual family, the Light of Jesus, all over the world. Parents need to be taught how to disciple their kids.

Frankly, I believe families weren't designed by God to live in isolation. Each family needs a "family of families."

Your Spiritual Life Needs a Team, Too

People aren't experiencing real Church life in a typical parish.

Most parishes are sacramental gas stations. People go in, gas up and go out. I don't think this was the original design for the Church.

To grow in our spiritual life, we need a team of mentors, peers and customers, too.

Mentors would be our priests, pastors and preachers.

But I'm very biased for a small group of friends to encourage you, inspire you and pray for you. That's where real discipleship happens. In small groups, a mentor disciples you. And your peers support you.

Small groups come in different names: cell groups, households, love circles, caring groups, home cells and support groups. It doesn't matter what name. As long as there's love and good food, it's what you need.

Hey, you even need "customers" or people whom you can serve.

Chapter 12

Long-Term Success Can Only Come from Teams

I repeat: Life is a team sport.

Look at David.

He defeated Goliath single-handedly.

But when he became a King, he had to build a faithful team of men around him — or his victory would be a one-shot deal.

So here's a key lesson: You can win a battle by yourself. But you cannot win a war unless you build a team.

Friend, are you tired of short-term wins that don't last?

Build a team. Long-term success can only come from a team.

Let me tell you a story about David's team.[10]

The Bible mentions three mighty men who served with David. They are Josheb-basshebeth, Eleazar and Shammah. (I have a feeling the first guy's mother loved tongue twisters like "she sells sea shells on the seashore.")

During that time, the Philistines were encamped in Bethlehem, David's birthplace.

---

[10] 2 Samuel 23:8-11, 14-17

One day, out of the blue, David said longingly, "Oh, I wish someone would give me water to drink from Bethlehem's well."

He wasn't saying it to anyone in particular.

It was just a sigh. He was just homesick.

Take note: "I want to drink water from Bethlehem's well" was like saying today, "I want to drink water from Al-Qaeda's camp in Afghanistan."

But Josheb, Eleazar and Shammah overheard David's sigh.

And they made it happen.

These three warriors gate-crashed the enemy's camp in Bethlehem to draw water from its well. I don't know how they did it. Perhaps like Indiana Jones, they fought their way in and fought their way out. Or they tiptoed around the camp while everyone was asleep. Or they borrowed Harry Potter's invisible cape. The Bible doesn't say. All it says is that the three guys survived and went back to David with his desired water.

That's the kind of team he had.

Tough. Loyal. Crazy.

David must have been a great leader to get that kind of loyalty.

You know the quality of your leadership by the quality of the team around you.

No wonder David was able to do much in his lifetime.

He had a Dream Team around him.

Chapter 13

Recruit People
Better than Yourself

"Bo, why are you so successful?"

I've been asked that question many times.

There are many ways to answer that question.

"Because I look like Brad Pitt" crosses my mind but I'm sure you want something more substantial.

Here's one of my favorite answers: *I look for people who are better than I am and I invite them to join my team.*

In other words, I've got a Dream Team that's out of this world.

I've met leaders who will always hire "smaller" people. Those whom they can boss around. Those whom they can intimidate easily. They cannot hire people who think on their own and can be mavericks. These strong-type leaders (who are really insecure and weak inside) cannot build a long-lasting organization. Once they disappear, the organization disappears with them.

When you form a team, always hire people better than you are.

That's why I love my team.

They're better than I am. Better leaders. Better preachers. Better organizers. Better in their various core gifts.

I lead nine non-profit organizations doing the wildest work on planet Earth, from exciting discipleship and media evangelism to dynamic ministries for the poorest of the poor.

Believe me, nothing happens in our ministries without a team!

And let me tell you something really amazing: The original team who led Light of Jesus with me, the first organization we built, is still serving with me after 30 years together.

It's true.

My wealth isn't in my bank account.

My wealth is in my address book.

My wealth is the wonderful friends who serve God with me.

I am truly blessed.

Chapter 14

Building a Team Is All About Relationships

Heard the line, "It's lonely at the top"?

For fake leaders, yes, this is true.

But not for real leaders.

Because real leaders are relationship experts.

In other words, real leaders love their team members. For them, it's never lonely at the top.

I consider my fellow leaders in my organizations as my family.

Hey, I even consider my driver and house helpers as my team! (For my foreign readers, I must explain. I'm not ultra-rich. In the Philippines, most middle-class families have helpers and drivers. It's very typical.)

My driver doesn't only work for me. I disciple him. I meet him regularly to discuss his spiritual, family and financial life.

I also try to promote our domestic helpers. If they want to study, I send them to school. Recently, one of our helpers got her college degree and now works as my staff assistant.

I teach our helpers to grow financially, too. I taught one of them to invest in the stock market and our other helper invests in a Euro mutual fund. Cool, huh?

More than paying them well, we treat them like family.

But no one beats Auring on how to treat helpers. Auring is a fiftyish woman who told me that her helper has been with her for 28 years. She says she's so lucky with her helper. But I'm sure the helper is saying the same thing.

If Auring goes to the beauty parlor to have her hair done, the helper also goes to have her hair done. If Auring goes through a mammography exam, the helper goes through a mammography exam, too.

In other words, Auring loves her helper.

Do you have a Dream Team?

Key #5

Take Action

It's True: God Helps Those Who Help Themselves!

Nothing happens unless something moves.
— Albert Einstein

Chapter 15

Have a Bias for Action

I'm about to share with you the Ten Sacred Rules of
Success.

Before I show it to you, I must warn you that this isn't
easy reading. It's deeply esoteric. If you have a difficult
time understanding it, don't panic. Don't be hard on
yourself. Not many can absorb it at the first reading. You'll
have to go through it perhaps 10 times before you absorb
its true genius.

These Ten Sacred Rules of Success came from
an ancient manuscript discovered in a hidden cave in
Northern China. It was used by the five martial arts
masters known at that time — Crane, Monkey, Tiger, Snake
and Praying Mantis.

Curious?

Turn the page and I'll show them to you...

Ten Sacred Rules of Success

Rule #1: Act.
Rule #2: Act again.
Rule #3: Act again.
Rule #4: Act again.
Rule #5: Act again.
Rule #6: Act again.
Rule #7: Act again.
Rule #8: Act again.
Rule #9: Act again.
Rule #10: Act again.

The guy who wrote it?
Kung Fu Panda.[11]
OK, I'm pulling your leg.
But it was fun presenting it to you this way.

Trust Is Better than Doing Nothing

My friend told me, "Bo, why is it that when you dream of something, I see it happen a few months later?"

"What?" I asked.

"One day, you tell me that you want to have a simple daily Bible reflection guide where ordinary people write their stories. Six months later, I see *Didache* in the bookstore. Another day, you tell me that you want to have a ministry for the poor. Six months later, Anawim is built on a five-hectare property. I don't get it. When you dream, it happens. When I dream, nothing happens."

I nodded, "My friend, it's simple. I have a bias for action."

---

[11] Just kidding. It's a Dreamworks movie. I have little boys so we watch lots of them.

"A bias for action?"

"Yes, I like doing things right away. Even when I make a mistake. I just act again and again and again…"

"Even if you're not sure?" he asked. "Sometimes, I'd get this great idea, but I get scared because I don't know what to do next."

I laughed. "Many times, I don't know what to do next either. Martin Luther King Jr. said, 'Take the first step in faith. You don't have to see the whole staircase.'"

My friend asked, "Does that work?"

I added, "I've realized that when I take action, the blessings of the universe flow to me. The right people, the right opportunities and the right resources come my way."

"So you trust?"

I smiled. "Yes, I trust. Believe me, it's better than doing nothing."

Chapter 16

Take Bold, Massive Action

Do you know what's common among the heroes of the Bible?

They took bold and massive action.

Noah built an ark.

Abraham migrated his family.

Joseph interpreted dreams.

Moses freed slaves.

Joshua conquered kings.

Ruth served Naomi.

Elijah dueled with gods.

Daniel silenced lions.

Judith beheaded the enemy.

Esther blessed a nation.

I could go on and on.

These men and women did great things for God because they were men and women of action.

Author Robert Ringer said, "The bolder the action, the greater the genius, magic and power that is likely to flow from it."

That's the spirituality we need to have.

Take on a Spirituality That Encourages Action

Some approaches to the spiritual life discourage action.

I learned this when I started preaching as a teenager.

After giving a talk on "God helps those who help themselves," a middle-aged man came up to me and said, "Young man, I don't agree with what you said. Do you know that the line 'God helps those who help themselves' isn't in the Bible?"

Being a "kid," I could only say, "I'm sorry, sir."

He explained, "The greatest sin of mankind is self-sufficiency. That we think we can do it without God. And you're teaching people to do that."

Oh, my God. What have I done? "I'm sorry, sir," I said again.

He continued, "Before I came to know God, I was a proud man. I made my own plans. Now, I just let Him lead me. As Spirit-led Christians, we should depend totally on the Holy Spirit. God doesn't help those who help themselves. God helps those who are helpless."

"Thank you, sir," I told the man.

I was sincere. I was floored by his words.

Such a holy man, I said.

But after a few more years of living on Planet Earth, I began to bump into a common problem among religious people: They were too passive. They lacked initiative. They didn't have a take-charge attitude that's so important in achieving great success.

Many of them were stuck in mediocrity. In their careers. In their family lives. Even in their ministries.

The problem? Overspiritualization.

They want God to do everything for them.

They don't even want to think or plan — they just want God to dictate to them what to do. They don't want to take initiative, lest they move before God.

If this is how God wants us to operate, why in the world did He give us a brain? Why did He give us imagination? Why did He give us creativity?

That was when I realized the line, "God helps those who help themselves," was a fantastic truth even if it wasn't specifically stated in the Bible. (Come to think of it, is trigonometry in the Bible? But my high school teacher really believes it works.)

I believe that "God helps those who help themselves" agrees with the spirit of the Bible's message.

Remember what the man told me as a teen? About the sin of self-sufficiency? About God helping the helpless?

It really doesn't contradict action.

While you act, totally trust Him.

Imagine If David Was Overspiritualized

Thank God David wasn't overspiritualized.

Because if he had been, this would have happened...

One day, he's tending sheep when he sees a prowling lion from the distance, hiding behind the rocks.

He closes his eyes and prays, "Lord, rescue my sheep. Perform a miracle, oh God. Strike that lion dead with a lightning bolt from the sky."

After a few seconds, he peeks to see that the lion is crawling nearer.

"Oh Lord, You're not doing anything. Do You want me to fight the lion myself? If You do, show me a sign." After thinking a bit, David says, "Lord, show me a red rose..."

He scans the horizon. He doesn't see a red rose, no

matter where he looks. David forgot he lived in the Judean wilderness where there are no roses for a thousand miles.

In the meantime, the hungry lion pounces on one poor lamb.

"Oh no, Lord," he gasps. "I asked for a red rose; not red blood." In desperation, he pulls out his Bible and closes his eyes. "Lord, I'm going to cut the Bible." With his eyes closed, he opens a page at random...

As he reads, the lion grabs another lamb.

I know this is an unfair caricature. But I'm driving my point across: There are times in your life when there's an urgency to act with boldness. Author Robert Allen said, "Everything you want is just outside your comfort zone."

Go ahead. Act. And act again. (Remember the Ten Sacred Secrets of Success?)

And make your dream come true.

Chapter 17

See Everything as Preparation

For the first 20 years of my ministry, I preached all over the place. Call me up and I'd pick up my Bible and go.

I didn't say no to any invitation.

One day, I received a call to give a talk to a school in Zambales. I was only 15 years old.

After a five-hour trip up north, I arrived. I met the nun who had invited me. She said, "Brother Bo, the kids are waiting for you."

"Sister, how long will my talk be?" I asked.

"From 9 a.m. to 3 p.m.," she said.

Gulp. Six hours?

"OK, Sister. By the way, how many kids will I speak to?"

"One thousand four hundred children. Grades 4, 5 and 6."

Double gulp.

She led me to a hot, sweltering gym where I saw a huge crowd of kids already bored to death even before I began. This wasn't going to be easy.

That day, I preached for six hours.

And that day, I learned to be a wild speaker. I had to say every joke, sing every song, tell every story, and jump, dance and eat fire — just to capture their attention.

Friend, if you want to be a great public speaker, talk to kids.

Because when you give a talk to adults, they're very respectful. If you become boring, they'll still listen to you. They'll even hide their yawns. After your boring talk, they'll even shake your hand and tell you they learned a lot.

Not kids. If you're boring for two seconds, they'll fly paper planes in front of you. They'll play *patintero*. Or they'll simply shout, "Boring!"

Friend, the first 20 years of my preaching days were all preparation. God was training me for bigger things.

Your Future Awaits

For years, David was a shepherd.

It was a thankless job. Aside from the fact that it was difficult and dangerous.

But David was faithful to that crummy job.

Because he was faithful, watching sheep prepared him for fighting a giant and ruling a nation.

Friend, are you going through a rough time today?

Do you feel you're stuck in a place you don't want to be?

I'm telling you: See everything as preparation.

Believe that everything that is happening to you today is training you for your great tomorrow.

Take the training.

Learn all you can.

Your future awaits.

Key #6

Fail Forward

There's Only One Road to Success — And This Is It!

The fellow who never makes a mistake takes his orders from one who does.

Chapter 18

Learn to Fail Forward

Have you failed in the past?

Many people know of only one kind of failure.

Actually, there are two kinds of failures.

You can fail backward or you can fail forward.

According to leadership expert John Maxwell, there's only one big difference between achievers and non-achievers. It's not talents, or background, or education. *It's how you respond to failure.* If you respond positively to failure, you become an achiever. If you respond negatively to failure, you become a non-achiever.

That's it!

According to studies made, successful entrepreneurs have 3.8 business failures before they actually succeed. And billionaires had to fail an average of 18 times before they hit their big wealth.

But we have a problem.

Our Problem: We're Not Trained to Fail

In school and at home, we're taught to fear failure.

We're taught to be depressed when we fail. We're taught that to succeed in life, we need to avoid failure at all costs.

Wrong training! Wrong education!

In school and at home, you're taught to avoid mistakes.

But in real life, you need to make mistakes to find what works.

In school and at home, you're punished when you fail.

But in real life, you must fail and fail and fail until you win.

In school and at home, you're trained to be book-smart.

But in real life, you need to be street-smart.

In school, you're trained to stay in line.

But in real life, you need to get out of your comfort zone.

Let me tell you something that shocked me.

Sweden has been recognized as having the best education system in the world. But would you believe that in their system, they have no tests in school?

Yes, they have exercises but they're encouraged to fail. The teacher says, "Hi, kids. Answer these questions to the best of your ability. If you fail, we'll take the exercise again until you learn."

Isn't that cool? This is one reason why we homeschool our kids. We apply the same principle when we teach our kids.[12]

By the way, have you noticed this?

Every time you attend class reunions, the people who used to have the highest grades are not necessarily the most successful people in the batch. The most successful may be the students who were average in their grades but who were experts in failing forward.

---

[12] For more information, you can log on to www.CatholicFilipinoAcademy.com

Homes need to be a safe place for failure, too.

A Mother Who Didn't Frown on Failure

I don't know where I read this story, but I love it.

One day, a little boy got the milk bottle from the fridge.

But because his hands were small, the milk bottle slipped and fell, creating a swimming pool of milk on the floor.

He quickly looked at his mother, expecting to be scolded.

But the mother was a wise woman.

She walked towards him and said calmly, "My, that's a great puddle of milk. Do you want to play in it for a while?"

The boy was surprised. After dipping his fingers in the milk and making little ripples for a few minutes, his mother then said, "Whoever makes a mess must clean it up." So they clean it together with a rag.

After that, she said, "Let's go to the backyard and learn how to carry a milk bottle with your two hands." So they went to the backyard. Mom filled the bottle with water and they began to practice...

That is what I mean by teaching our kids to fail forward.

You don't scold them for trying. Trying is good. Don't squash their desire to try. That's the only way they'll learn in real life.

In fact, you need to train your kids to prepare for failure.

Chapter 19

Be Prepared for Failure

Did you notice?

When David faced Goliath, he didn't pick one stone.

He picked five stones.

I love that.

Because he expected to fail.

And with each failure, he knew he'd learn how *not* to throw a stone. He would know how to change the angle, or the speed, or the trajectory.

Mary Kay Ash, founder of a cosmetic empire, said, "For every failure, there's an alternative course of action. You just have to find it. When you come to a roadblock, take a detour."

Some religious people I know think they're exempted from taking detours. They want God to guide them to a perfect path. Because they believe that God will protect them from failures. That's not true! Here's why: If God protects you from failures, then He'll be protecting you from His greatest gifts — wisdom, spiritual growth and His redirection.

I agree with playwright J.M. Barrie when he said, "We are all failures. At least, the best of us are."

Do you want to be the best?

Then you have to fail.

The Two Rocks of Great Wisdom

On top of a high mountain, an excited young man knocked on the door of an isolated hut. When an old monk opened the door, the young man bowed low and said, "My name is Solomon. I know many things of God already as other holy men have trained me. But I wish to learn more. I've heard that you can teach me. Can you train me in the ways of God?"

The older monk obliged and the young man was very happy.

For the next six months, the elderly man taught Solomon a most important skill: that of *prayerful labor,* or the ability to pray while working. Both men would walk together down the mountain path, buy bread in the market and distribute it to the beggars in the village. All the while, the old man challenged Solomon to commune with God in his heart while he served the poor.

But alas, after six months, Solomon was very discouraged. Because he couldn't connect with God. He couldn't pray while surrounded by the noise of the beggars. And he kept getting irritated by their ways. He felt like a total failure.

Solomon went to the older man, and with a sad voice said, "Master, I have failed. I will go home and give up."

The grey-haired monk smiled. "Finally, your training is now about to begin. Congratulations."

The young man scratched his head. "I don't get it, Master. I've been training for six months."

The old man went to his room and came out carrying a wooden chest. He opened it and said, "I'm about to give you the two Rocks of Great Wisdom. All learning comes from these two Rocks. Are you ready?"

Solomon nodded and opened his palms.

On the young man's right hand, the old monk placed a white rock. The student looked at it and saw the inscription, "There are no failures, only lessons."

The older monk said, "That is why I told you that your training begins only today. For six months, you were full of yourself. Now, because of failure, you're empty and ready to learn. If you learn this first Rock of Great Wisdom, you can be discouraged, but never be crushed by anything ever again."

On his student's left hand, the old man placed a black rock.

The apprentice read the inscription on the second rock. "A lesson is repeated until it is learned."

The old man said, "Failing for six months means you're a student. Failing for 60 years means you're simply stubborn."

Without a word, Solomon walked out of the hut and shut the door behind him.

A few minutes later, a knock was heard.

When the old monk opened the door, there was a young man at the door.

He bowed low and said, "My name is Solomon. I do not know anything and I'm ready to fail. Can you train me in the ways of God?"

Don't Fail to Get the Golden Goose

There are no failures, only lessons.

Remember that every time you fail, you're given a lesson. This lesson is like a golden goose that will lay a golden egg into your hands every day.

It's the foolish people who don't pick up their golden goose from their failures. They will fail again because *lessons are repeated until they are learned*.

Champions fail all the time.

They just know how to profit from their failures.

Chapter 20

Feel the Fear
but Fail Anyway

Someone gave me the "History of All Successes in the World" — and I love it. Every success usually goes through five stages.

Here they are:

Stage 1: You're afraid to look foolish.

Stage 2: You look foolish.

Stage 3: You're actually foolish!

Stage 4: You gradually become successful.

Stage 5: You're called a genius.

It's normal to be afraid (Stage 1). Because you don't want to look foolish (Stage 2). And you don't want to *be* foolish (Stage 3).

It's OK. Feel the fear.

Everyone goes through it, even the best champions.

But do what you've got to do anyway. So that you can experience the victory of Stage 5.

Please remember: Short-term failure isn't failure. *Short-term failure is the only pathway to long-term success.*

Remember that as Christians, we're saved by the greatest failure in the history of the world: The Cross.

Allow yourself to fail. In fact, allow yourself to fail greatly. It was President Robert F. Kennedy who said,

"Only those who dare to fail greatly can ever achieve greatly."

Will you dare to fail greatly?

Novel writer Ray Bradbury has this funny line that describes my life: "Living at risk is jumping off the cliff and building your wings on the way down." Believe me, I've jumped off a cliff many times.

Like when we launched *Kerygma* magazine for the first time and ran out of money after six months.

And when we built Anawim, our ministry for the poorest of the poor. Believe me, we had so many problems with staff and systems (or the lack of them), I got depressed. I no longer knew how to solve our problems. But funny, I didn't label what I felt as depression. I also didn't know that depression dulled one's senses. So as I drove home late one night, I crashed my car into a delivery van. Reason? I didn't see it at all. That woke me up and made me realize I was actually depressed.

I also remember how we started one TV show after another, and how we had to cancel after one or two seasons. We pulled it off the air, reformatted and launched again. We failed four times!

Oh, I could go on and on and write a really thick book about my failures. But it's because of these many failures that we're incredibly successful today.

Friend, give yourself permission to fail.

When you do, you give yourself permission to succeed.

Key #7

Shine Your Light

Be Humble by Serving the World

*"In the same way, let your light shine before men,
that they may see your good deeds and praise your
Father in heaven."*
— Jesus Christ

Chapter 21

Heal Your Success Acrophobia

Very few people are afflicted with acrophobia.

Acrophobia is the fear of heights. People with acrophobia can't look down when they're on top of a building. I bet some of them can't wear the high heels of Jennifer Lopez, either.

But *more* people are afflicted with success acrophobia — the fear of worldly, material, professional success.

These people, in a subconscious way, avoid it.

Where does success acrophobia come from?

1. Cultural Roots

As I go around the world, I'm amazed at how prevalent these limiting beliefs are. They're everywhere.

Here are common sayings from four countries:

Japan: "The nail that sticks up gets hammered down."

England: "Don't be behaving like a big Mick."

USA: "Don't get too big for your britches."

Philippines: *"Pag hindi ka kinakausap, manahimik ka."*[13]

---

[13] "If you're not being spoken to, keep quiet."

2. Religious Roots

Some religious people think that self-hatred is a prerequisite for sainthood. For them, holy people should love God and despise themselves. Holy people should punish their bodies. Holy people should shun all forms of pride — even healthy pride — as part of the Seven Cardinal Sins. After all, pride caused Lucifer to fall.

They forget a very important fact: That self-hatred is still being self-centered. I like what William Temple, archbishop of Canterbury, said about humility. He said, "Humility does not mean thinking less of yourself than of other people, nor does it mean having a low opinion of your own gifts. It means freedom from thinking about yourself at all."

More on humility on the next chapter.

3. Family Roots

Our beliefs are shaped by our families of origin.

One day, after giving my *How to Be Truly Rich* seminar, a middle-aged man came up to me crying. He said, "Thank you, Bo, for giving me permission to seek success."

He explained, "As a boy, my parents drilled into me that to seek success is greed. They told me that if I were to be successful, it would just happen. Because God will make it happen. They taught me not to seek it or I might lose my soul. So all my life, I feel I've been stuck. Financially, I can't make ends meet. Would you believe? I even turn down promotions thinking they're bad."

If you were taught that money was evil, you'll avoid it. If you were taught that rich people are thieves, you'll avoid becoming rich.

But sometimes, parents don't have to say the words, "Success is bad." They just have to show it to you.

I met a beautiful girl who had very successful parents. They were very rich and accomplished. Unfortunately, they were also very cold and distant towards their daughter. To her, they lived lives of hypocrisy — happy on the outside, miserable on the inside.

In a subconscious way, when she grew up, this young woman avoided anything that smelled of success. Perhaps this was the reason why she married a poor man and left high society because she connected success with misery, emptiness and hypocrisy.

What Did You Hear More Frequently?

I'll give two sets of statements. Tell me which set you heard more while growing up at home:

Set A
• Who do you think you are?
• Don't toot your own horn.
• Don't be too proud of yourself.
• Don't be a know-it-all.
• Don't stand out.
• Be seen and not heard.
• Be quiet unless you're asked to speak.
• Don't aim too high.
• It's better to remain small and hidden.

Set B
- You can be anything you want to be.
- You've got what it takes to succeed.
- You're a phenomenal person.
- Think big.
- Reach for the stars.
- Be seen *and* heard.
- Be proud of who you are.
- Aim high!
- Go for it!

I've asked these questions in my talks. It's sad that more people grew up hearing Set A rather than Set B.

I invite you now to change your definition of humility.

Chapter 22

Redefine Humility

One day, I brought my son Bene with me to a doctor's clinic.

While in the waiting room, he read a book beside me.

One lady in the waiting room asked him, "How old are you?"

Bene said, "I'm four years old."

"Oh my!" the woman said. "And you can read that book?" It was a book for eight-year-olds.

Bene answered, "Yes, I started reading when I was three years old. I'm a very good reader."

The lady answered, "And I see you're also very humble."

The other people in the waiting room who were listening to the conversation laughed.

Bene didn't laugh. Because he didn't get the joke.

And that was a good thing.

When he gets older, he would get the joke: That it's not acceptable to tell people your talents and be proud of them. Because good people don't do that. Because good people are humble.

What Is Humility Anyway?

People are so confused about humility.

Let me straighten the record for you.
- Humility is not shyness.
- Humility is not being quiet.
- Humility is not being timid.
- Humility is not having low self-worth.
- Humility is not being a wallflower.
- Humility is not being fearful.
- Humility is not being coy.
- Humility is not being tentative.
- Humility is not being faint-hearted.

What is humility then?

Two words: *Selfless servanthood.*

That's it.

I believe humility is the secret to success.

When you serve others, you plant seeds of greatness that will return to you a hundredfold. Saint Augustine said, "Do you wish to rise? Begin by descending. You plan a tower that will pierce the clouds? Lay first the foundation of humility."

For David, delivering lunch to his brothers and fighting a giant were one and the same thing: He came to serve.

In order to do that, he had to "advertise" himself when he faced the King. He spoke of his accomplishments. Not very humble in today's definition. He told the King, "You can send me to Goliath. I know I can kill him because I've terminated a few bad lions and bears before."

If David had *false* humility, he wouldn't have even volunteered.

Or if he did, he would have said something like this: "King Saul, you can, but I'm not forcing you to send me to Goliath. I did some things in the past that may qualify me for the job but I'd rather not mention them. I don't want to boast. I believe I can defeat Goliath, though, of course I may be wrong…"

Here's what I believe: Every person, business and organization's ultimate mission is to serve others.

Sometimes, though, you have to advertise your services.

If you want to serve, you shouldn't be ashamed to show people your strength. Go ahead, advertise yourself. Tell the world about the gift that God gave you. Because your intention isn't to lift yourself up, but to lift up those you want to serve.

Chapter 23

Be Confident When You Shine Your Light

Motivational speaker Zig Ziglar said, "Timid salesmen have skinny kids."

I agree.

Imagine buying something from a not-very-confident salesman. I can assure you it will be very frustrating.

Salesman: "Sir, would you, uh, like to buy this, uh, car?"

Buyer: "Is it good?"

Salesman: "Uhm, depending on how you look at it, it's OK."

Buyer: "Is it dependable?"

Salesman: "I may be wrong, but I guess it is."

Buyer: "If you were in my shoes, would you buy it?"

Salesman: "I'm not sure. Perhaps."

Tell me, will this salesman sell many cars?

I don't think so.

But I've noticed this is exactly how people sell themselves.

Here's the harsh truth: At every moment of your life, you are selling yourself. Your success depends on how confident you are in yourself.

Let me show you how you can grow in confidence:

1. How You Carry Yourself

If you slouch, dress sloppily and can't look people directly in the eye, people will know you lack confidence and may not take you seriously. If you stand up straight, dress smart and look people in the eye, people will give you respect.

I've got a little secret to tell you. (Public speakers, take note.) There are times when I feel lousy before I give a talk. Perhaps I woke up on the wrong side of the bed. Perhaps I feel tired because I slept late. Perhaps I'm carrying a burden.

As a speaker, you can't bring that with you to the stage. Your audience deserves a speaker brimming with joy and excitement.

So here's what I do. *I pretend I'm feeling great.*

I act as if I'm confident.

I stand up straight, I tilt my head high, I smile a confident smile and I take a deep breath.

Instantly, I feel better. No kidding.

And I give a superb talk.

Change your physiology and you change your psychology.

2. How You Speak about Yourself to Others

When I ask people what they do, they say things like…

"Not much. I'm just a plain housewife."

"Oh, I'm only a clerk."

"I'm just a security guard."

When someone answers in this way, he's telling me that he's not proud of what he does.

I've got a suggestion.

If you're a housewife, say this instead: "I'm a full-time wife and mother, raising my children to become phenomenal human beings."

And if you're a clerk, say this: "I'm in charge of assisting the head of our department fulfill his goals and make our entire office run smoothly."

And if you're a security guard, say this: "I'm responsible for protecting and safeguarding our 200-million-peso factory and all its assets."

Unless you're a thief or a smuggler, don't ever look down on what you do.

One day, an old lady who had never read any of my books, asked me point-blank, "Do you write well?"

Our funny culture dictates that I should answer, *"Naku, hindi naman"* (Not really). But I answered instead, "I love writing, and yes, I do write very well. It's my passion."

Believe me, a confident answer is so much better — for you and for the other person.

3. How to Speak to Yourself about Yourself

I've met people who berate themselves constantly. Their favorite pastime is to criticize themselves. All they do is pick at their faults constantly.

One day, I caught a young woman doing this. She hit her head with her fist while saying, "Stupid! Stupid! Stupid!"

I asked her, "Do you do that often?"

"Do what?" she asked.

I said, "Hit yourself on the head and say *stupid* three times."

"Oh that," she said. "That's because this stupid girl made a big blunder," pointing to her work.

"There you go again, calling yourself stupid."

"Because I am," she said.

I said, "If you treated others the same way you treat yourself, I bet you would have been murdered a long time ago."

That made her laugh.

I explained, "The most important conversation you will ever have is your conversation with yourself. Don't put yourself down, even if you make mistakes. Affirm yourself."

"How, Bo?" she asked. "I've always been like this."

So I taught her five affirmations to say every day.

1. "God is with me."
2. "I'm a gifted person."
3. "I'm a winner. I'm a successful person."
4. "I'm a great husband (wife). I'm a fantastic father (mother)."
5. "I'm very wealthy. I'm very generous."

I told her, "You become the labels you give yourself. So have a healthy pride in who you are. When you don't celebrate who you are, you lack gratitude for the One who made you."

Write these statements on a card and post it on your wall.

Or put it on your computer screen.

Or make it the screensaver on your cell phone.

Just keep saying it.

And you'll see the difference.

Say it often enough and your entire day will change.

Shine your light!

Epilogue

Win in the Most Important Battle of Your Life

If you miss love, you miss life.
— *Leo Buscaglia*

I waited for the end of the book to tell you this.

David may have won over Goliath.

David may have won over armies.

David may have won over Israel and became its king.

But there was a time in his life when David didn't conquer his lust. He fell into adultery with Bathsheba and killed her husband, Uriah. It was an ugly story. Ultimately, he asked for forgiveness. I thank God that the Bible didn't cover up the bad stuff.

Because it teaches us a very critical lesson. David had a lot of military victories but he lost when it came to the most important battle of life: following his inner compass.

You have an inner compass that will guide you to happiness.

This inner compass always points to a spiritual north.

Friend, your spiritual north will always be love.

This is the battle that you must win.

It involves your most important relationships.

If You Fail in Your Relationships, You Fail in Life

One day, I prayed for a huge man in the hospital.

The man was an athlete with a superb physical condition. As a weightlifter, he lifted 300 pounds without much sweat. Everything in his body was in excellent condition — his muscles, his bones, his lungs, his kidneys…. Everything, that is, except his heart.

He was a dying man. Because his heart was dying.

Your relationships are the heart of your life.

You can be winning in your business, in your profession, in your finances or even in your health. But if you fail in your relationships, you fail in life.

If you fail in love, you fail in all things.

Make a choice now to live a life of love.

Be a champion.

Most of all, be a Champion of Love.

May your dreams come true,

Bo Sanchez
bosanchez@kerygmafamily.com

P.S. *A champion is a doer.* Go back and review the book. Look at what you underlined and the notes you put on the margins. Choose one thing that you'll do *now*. Then do it. And then tell me about it.

P.S.2. Get my tiny *Novena to God's Love* **and the** *Life Dreams and Success Journal.* Both are mailed totally FREE to those who support our ministry. Log on to **www. kerygmafamily.com** and receive a mountain load of FREE resources for your personal growth.

About the Author

Bo Sanchez is a preacher, leader and entrepreneur. He is the author of over 30 bestselling books and publisher of eight periodicals. Bo also has a weekly TV show, a daily radio program and a daily Internet TV show. He travels extensively around the world as a powerful speaker. So far, he has addressed audiences in 14 countries, including 36 cities in North America.

He founded many organizations, such as Anawim, a special home for the abandoned elderly, and Shepherd's Voice, a media group that publishes the widest read inspirational literature in the country. He is also the founder of the Light of Jesus Family, a spiritual community.

He was also cited as one of The Outstanding Young Men (TOYM) in 2006.

Privately, Bo is a successful entrepreneur. He frequently teaches and writes about financial literacy, believing that poverty is hugely a product of people's low financial I.Q., He focuses on subjects such as debt management, saving, investing and business.

In another endeavor he's very passionate about, Bo started the Catholic Filipino Academy **(www. catholicfilipinoacademy.com)** to help parents who want to homeschool their children.

But above all these, Bo believes that his first call is to be a loving husband to his wife, Marowe, and a devoted father to his sons, Benedict and Francis. They live in Manila, Philippines.

For more information, log on to his website **www. bosanchez.ph** or email him at **bosanchez@kerygmafamily. com.**